P9-DUB-910

Norman Rockwell Bookplate

Norman Rockwell's bookplate, c. 1925. Pen and ink on paper. First edition copy in private collection.

Norman Rockwell

An American Tradition

An imprint of
RUNNING PRESS
Philadelphia, Pennsylvania

Copyright © 1988 Estate of Norman Rockwell.
All rights reserved under the Pan-American and International
Copyright Conventions.

This book may not be reproduced in whole or in part in any form
or by any means, electronic or mechanical, including photocopying,
recording, or by any information storage and retrieval system now
known or hereafter invented, without written permission
from the publisher.

Canadian representatives: General Publishing Co., Ltd.,
30 Lesmill Road, Don Mills, Ontario M3B 2T6.

International representatives: Worldwide Media Services, Inc.,
115 East Twenty-third Street, New York, NY 10010.

9   8   7   6   5   4   3   2   1

Digit on the right indicates the number of this printing.

Library of Congress Cataloging-in-Publication Number
88-70996

ISBN 0-89471-677-8
Cover design by Toby Schmidt.
Cover and title page illustration: *The Runaway* by Norman Rockwell.
Collection of the Norman Rockwell Museum at Stockbridge,
Stockbridge, Massachusetts. Copyright © 1958 by Estate of Norman
Rockwell, reproduced with permission.

Photographs for endpapers and Illustrations No. 1-21, 23-42,
44-60 courtesy of The Norman Rockwell Museum at Stockbridge,
Stockbridge, Massachusetts.

Illustration No. 22 courtesy of GE Lighting, Nela Park, Cleveland, Ohio.

Illustration No. 43 copyright © 1946 Brown and Bigelow. All rights
reserved. Produced from copyright art from the Archives of Brown
& Bigelow and with permission of the Boy Scouts of America.

Foreword excerpted from *The Norman Rockwell Postcard Book*
copyright © 1987 by Running Press Book Publishers.
Reprinted with permission.

Typography by Fidelity Graphics.
Printed and bound in Hong Kong.

Published by Courage Books, an imprint of
Running Press Book Publishers,
125 South Twenty-second Street, Philadelphia, PA 19103.

Contents

Foreword

With his affectionate portrayals of ordinary Americans, conceived with heartfelt good humor and painted in an almost photographically realistic style, Norman Rockwell recorded the everyday life of our nation for more than sixty years.

In 1916, when he was 21, he was working as an illustrator for children's magazines in New Rochelle, New York. That year he traveled to Philadelphia to offer three of his illustrations to the nation's largest mass-circulation magazine, *The Saturday Evening Post.* The art editor, to his credit, immediately recognized Rockwell's talent, accepted the three illustrations as covers for the *Post,* and asked for more. Thus began the long and happy association between Rockwell and the *Post,* for which Rockwell painted more than 300 covers.

Rockwell met and married Mary Barstow in 1930, and the couple had three sons. In 1939 the family moved to Arlington, Vermont, where Rockwell found inspiration for his work and discovered many of his neighbors to be "exactly the models I need for my purpose—the sincere, honest, homespun types that I love to paint."

When his studio burned to the ground in 1943, many of Rockwell's paintings were destroyed. The only record available today of many of Rockwell's works—including some reproduced in this book—are the *Post* covers themselves.

The Rockwell family moved to Stockbridge, Massachusetts, in 1953, where the artist converted an old carriage house into a studio. There he continued to paint with great enthusiasm and success until his death in 1978.

For the many Americans who recognize themselves in these closely observed moments of American life, Rockwell's paintings have come to represent a collective family album.

Part One
1910 to 1920

1.

2.

1. *The Magic Football*
   St. Nicholas, December, 1914, page 131. Illustration for "The
   Magic Football" by Ralph Henry Barbour. Oil on canvas.
   Norman Rockwell Paintings Trust at Old Corner House.

2. *Till the Boys Come Home*
   Life, August 15, 1918, cover. Oil on canvas. Private collection.

3. *The Little Mother*
   Life, November 7, 1918, cover. Oil on canvas. Private collection.

3.

THE LITTLE MOTHER

4.

4. *...But Wait til Next Week!*
   Country Gentleman, May 8, 1920, cover. Whereabouts unknown.

5.

5. *Retribution!*
   Country Gentleman, May 15, 1920, cover.

6.

6. *The Party Favor*
Saturday Evening Post, April 26, 1919, cover. Oil on canvas.
Private collection.

7.

7. *Is He Coming?*
   Life, December 16, 1920, cover. Oil on canvas. Private collection.

8.

8. *Grandpa Listening In on the Wireless*
   Literary Digest, February 21, 1920, cover. Oil on canvas. Private collection.

9.

9. *The Circus Barker (The Strongman)*
Saturday Evening Post, June 3, 1916, cover. Oil on canvas.
Collection of Curtis Publishing Company.

10.

10. *And the Symbol of Welcome Is Light*
    Lamp advertisement for Edison Mazda, 1920. Oil on canvas.
    Collection of General Electric Lighting Company, Cleveland.

Part Two
The 1920s

11.

12.

11. ***If Your Wisdom Teeth Could Talk They'd Say, "Use Colgate's"***

Advertisement for Colgate Dental Cream, 1924. Oil on canvas.
Old Corner House Collection, bequest of Mrs. George H. Sheldon.

12. ***Girl Reading Palm***

Saturday Evening Post, March 12, 1921, cover. Oil on canvas.
Private collection.

13. ***Home Sweet Home***

Life, August 23, 1923, cover.

13.

14.

15.

14. —*And Daniel Boone Comes to Life on the Underwood Portable*
Advertisement for Underwood typewriters, 1923. Oil on
canvas. Private collection.

15. *Boy Playing Flute Surrounded by Animals*
Saturday Evening Post, April 16, 1927, cover. Oil on canvas.
Private collection.

16.

16. *Christmas Trio*
   Saturday Evening Post, December 8, 1923, cover. Oil on board.
   Norman Rockwell Paintings Trust at Old Corner House.

17.

17. *Doctor and Doll*
    Saturday Evening Post, March 9, 1929, cover. Oil on canvas.
    Private collection.

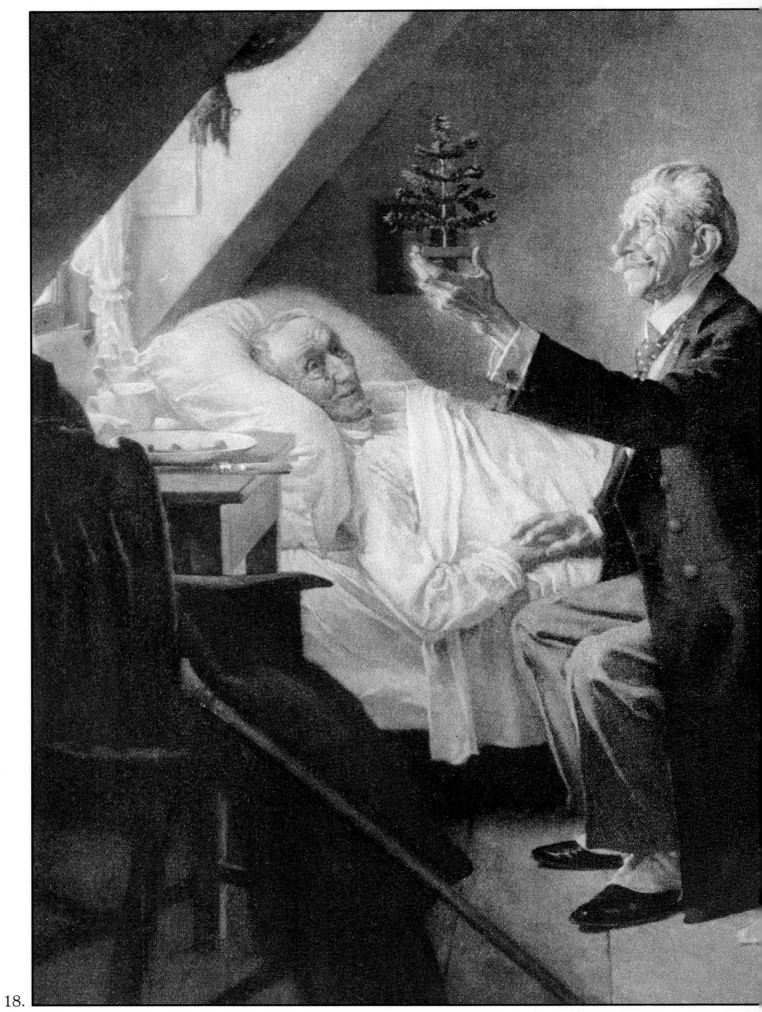

18.

19.

18. **A Christmas Reunion**
Ladies' Home Journal, December 1927, page 15. Oil on canvas.
Private collection.

19. **Downhill Racing Cart**
Saturday Evening Post, January 9, 1926, cover. Oil on canvas.
Private collection.

20.

20. **Pipe and Bowl Sign Painter**
Saturday Evening Post, February 6, 1926, cover. Oil on canvas.
Private collection.

21.

22.

21. *Checkers*

   Ladies' Home Journal, July 1929. Illustration for "With an
   Incident of the Circus as Remembered by Courtney Ryley
   Cooper," page 11. Oil on canvas. Old Corner House Collection.

22. ***Look at This Picture—Then Look at Your Light***
   Lamp advertisement for Edison Mazda, 1925. Oil on canvas.
   Collection of General Electric Lighting Company, Cleveland.

23.

23. *Fruit of the Vine*
Advertisement for Sun Maid raisins. Oil on canvas.
Private collection.

24.

24. *The Stay at Homes*
   Ladies' Home Journal, October, 1927, page 24. Oil on canvas.
   Norman Rockwell Paintings Trust at Old Corner House.

Part Three
The 1930s

25.

25. *The Land of Enchantment*
   Saturday Evening Post, December 22, 1934, pages 18-19. Oil on
   canvas. Collection of the New Rochelle Library.

26.

26. **Woman at Vanity (Girl Getting Ready for Date)**
Saturday Evening Post, October 21, 1933, cover. Oil on canvas.

27.

27. *Family Home from Vacation*
Saturday Evening Post, September 13, 1930, cover. Oil on canvas.
Private collection.

28.

29.

28. **Spring Tonic**
   Saturday Evening Post, May 30, 1936, cover. Oil on canvas.
   Private collection.

29. **Christmas: Santa Reading Mail**
   Saturday Evening Post, December 21, 1935, cover. Oil on canvas.
   Private collection.

30.

30. *Barbershop Quartet*

Saturday Evening Post, September 26, 1936, cover. Oil on canvas.
Private collection.

Part Four
The 1940s

31.

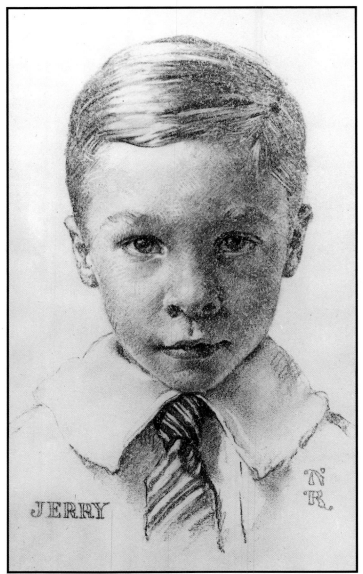

32.

31. *Portrait of Mary Barstow Rockwell*
   c. 1950. Charcoal on paper. Private collection.

32. *Portrait of Jerry Rockwell*
   c. 1940. Charcoal on paper. Private collection.

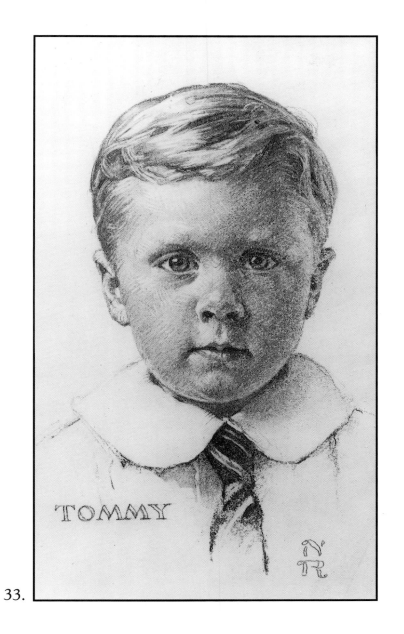

33.

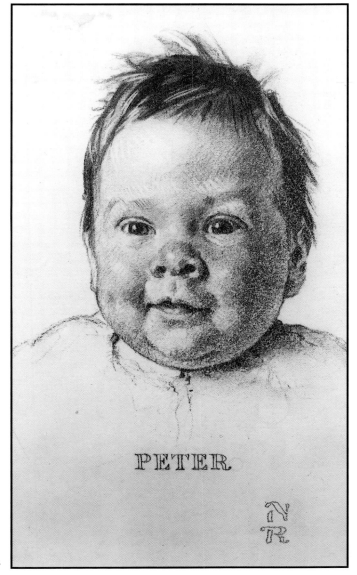

34.

33. *Portrait of Tommy Rockwell*
c. 1940. Charcoal on paper. Private collection.

34. *Portrait of Peter Rockwell*
c. 1940. Charcoal on paper. Private collection.

35.

35. *Strictly a Sharpshooter*
American Magazine, June, 1941. Illustration for "Strictly a
Sharpshooter" by D.D. Beauchamp, pages 40-41. Oil on canvas.
Old Corner House Collection.

36.

36. *Freedom of Speech*
   Saturday Evening Post, February 20, 1943. Illustration for
   "Freedom of Speech" by Booth Tarkington, page 85. Oil on
   canvas. Norman Rockwell Paintings Trust at Old Corner House.

37.

37. *Freedom to Worship*
   Saturday Evening Post, February 27, 1943. Illustration for
   "Freedom of Worship" by Will Durant, page 85. Oil on canvas.
   Norman Rockwell Paintings Trust at Old Corner House.

38.

39.

38. *Homecoming Marine*
Saturday Evening Post, October 13, 1945, cover. Oil on canvas.

39. *Thanksgiving: Mother and Son Peeling Potatoes*
Saturday Evening Post, November 24, 1945, cover. Oil on canvas.
Private collection.

40.

40. *The American Way*
    World War II poster for Disabled American Veterans, 1944.
    Oil. Collection of Disabled American Veterans.

41. ***Going and Coming***
   Saturday Evening Post, August 30, 1947, cover. Oil on canvas.
   Norman Rockwell Paintings Trust at Old Corner House.

42.

42. *Charwomen in Theater*
   Saturday Evening Post, April 6, 1946, cover. Oil on canvas.
   Private collection.

43.

43. *A Guiding Hand*
Calendar illustration for Boy Scouts of America, 1946.
Copyright © 1946 by Brown and Bigelow. All rights reserved.
Oil on canvas. Collection of National Office, Boy Scouts of America.

44.

44. *Norman Rockwell Visits a Family Doctor*
Saturday Evening Post, April 12, 1947. Illustration for "Norman
Rockwell Visits a Family Doctor," pages 30-31. Oil on canvas.
Old Corner House Collection.

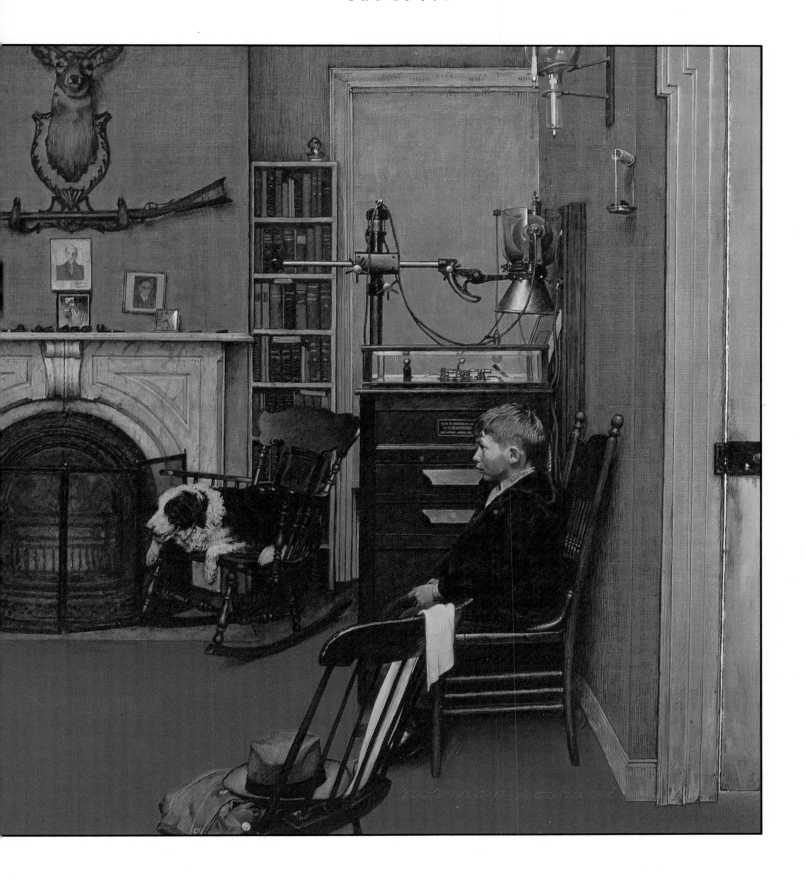

45.

45. *The Gossips*
    Saturday Evening Post, March 6, 1948, cover. Oil on canvas.
    Whereabouts unknown.

46.

46. *New Television Antenna*
   Saturday Evening Post, November 5, 1949, cover. Oil on canvas.
   Collection of the Los Angeles County Museum of Art.

47.

47. *April Fool: Girl with Shopkeeper*
    Saturday Evening Post, April 3, 1948, cover. Private collection.

Part Five
The 1950s and 1960s

48.

48. *The Problem We All Live With*
Look, January 14, 1964. Illustration for "The Problem We All Live With," pages 22-23. Oil on canvas. Old Corner House Collection.

49.

49. *Saying Grace*
Saturday Evening Post, November 24, 1951, cover. Oil on canvas.
Private collection.

50.

50. **"Oh Boy! It's Pop with a New Plymouth!"**
Advertisement for Plymouth automobiles, 1951. Oil on canvas.

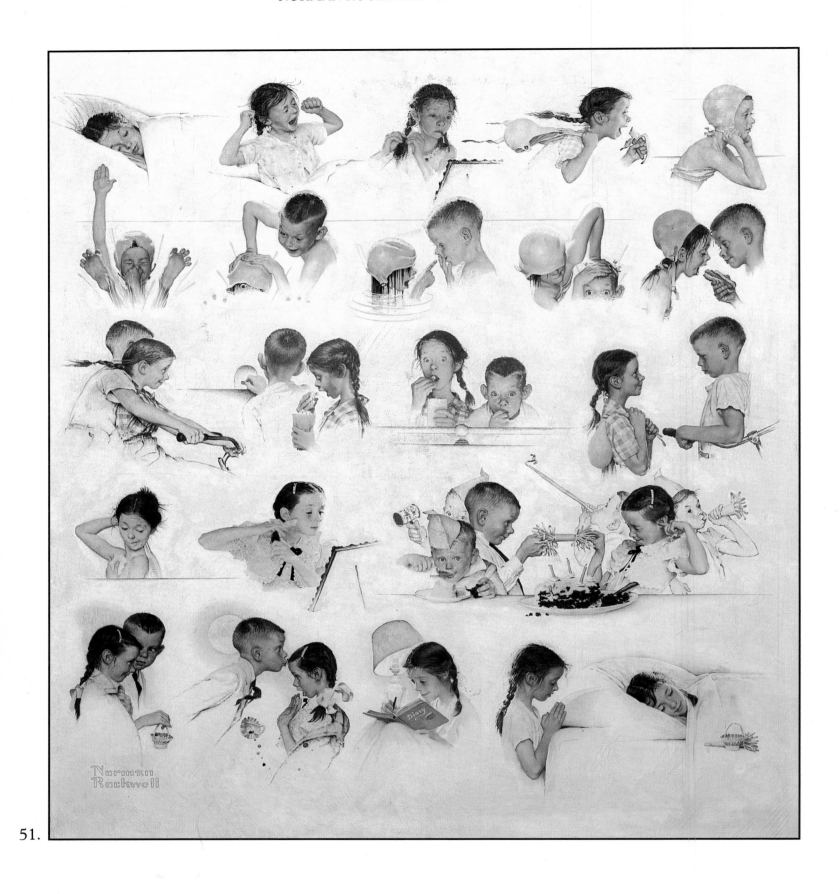

51.

51. *Day in the Life of a Little Girl*
Saturday Evening Post, August 30, 1952, cover. Oil on canvas.
Old Corner House Collection.

52.

52. *Girl With Black Eye*
Saturday Evening Post, May 23, 1953, cover. Oil on canvas.
Collection of the Wadsworth Atheneum.

53.

53. **Portrait of Norman Rockwell Painting the Soda Jerk**
    1953. Oil on board. Private collection.

54. **Shuffleton's Barbershop**
    Saturday Evening Post, April 29, 1950, cover. Oil on canvas.
    Collection of the Berkshire Museum.

56.

56. *After the Prom*
   Saturday Evening Post, May 25, 1957, cover. Oil on canvas.
   Private collection.

57.

57. *The Runaway*

Saturday Evening Post, September 20, 1958, cover. Oil on canvas.
Norman Rockwell Paintings Trust at Old Corner House.

58. *Willie Was Different*

Illustration for *Willie Was Different* by Molly and Norman
Rockwell, New York, Funk and Wagnalls, 1967, page 16. Oil on
board. Norman Rockwell Paintings Trust at Old Corner House.

58.

59.

59. *Man on the Moon*
   Look, January 10, 1967. Illustration for "Man on the Moon" by
   John Osmundson, pages 40-41. Oil on canvas. Collection of
   National Air and Space Museum, Smithsonian Institution.

60.

60. *Triple Self-Portrait*
   Saturday Evening Post, February 13, 1960, cover. Oil on canvas.
   Norman Rockwell Paintings Trust at Old Corner House.

Faithful Friend
Autograph sketch, pre-1950. Ink on paper. Private collection.